THE HORSE ORCHARD

Poems

FIONNA PERKINS

For Deborah Bruner, a meeting over the 80th anniversary, all best.
Fionna Perkins
August 26, 2000
Mendocino

Floreant Press
Forestville, California

Floreant Press
6195 Anderson Road
Forestville, California 95436

Printed in the USA by Floreant Press
10 9 8 7 6 5 4 3 2 1
First Printing

Perkins, Fionna
The Horse Orchard: Poems / by Fionna Perkins
-- 1st ed.
p. cm.
LCCN: 99-66172
ISBN: 0-9649497-2-5

1. Nature--Poetry. 2. Natural history--California, Northern--Poetry. 3. California, Northern--Poetry. I. Title.

PS3566.E691476Hor 2000 811'.54
QBI99-1432

Cover art by Marylu Downing
Cover Design: Carol Fussell
Title Page Photo: Bill Elliott Perry

In memory of

my parents

Ethel and Norman Sinclair

and for my husband

Richard

And everything comes to One,
As we dance on, dance on, dance on.

"Once More, the Round"
Theodore Roethke, 1908-1963

TABLE OF CONTENTS

INTRODUCTION

At Fionna and Richard Perkins' home near Anchor Bay, her shaggy Shetland and Welsh ponies meet you at the gate. They roam and browse from redwood groves to the Perkins' porch. Sea lions bark far down on rocks amid the crashing breakers of the Pacific surf. Fionna's long narrative, "The Horse Orchard," tells of a gallant black pony whose adventurous life ended at home during a fierce storm. The poem also narrates life on the Mendocino coast, endurance, love, a marriage that has spanned half a century, revelations and sadness, a recognition of time passing.

Fionna's life began in 1919 in the mountains of Montana. Her family, the Scottish Sinclairs, were not easily discouraged by rough conditions, but as hard times worsened, even they pulled up their roots and headed for the west. Fionna's childhood and adolescence took place during the Depression, in places far from town. As an isolated, youngest child, she escaped into nature and reading. She loved animals, especially horses, which she yearned to ride fast to somewhere, anywhere, far away. She was hungry for learning. All her life she has felt books and places to talk about books with others were necessary to a good life. In the early sixties, Fionna opened the first bookstore on the Mendocino coast. Over the decades, she has organized readings, helped put out local poets' chapbooks, and given thousands of hours of her time to make sure a new library for readers in her remote, rugged area gets built. She won't cancel a reading or a radio show for gale-force winds, floods, even a run-in with a deer.

Fionna Perkins is truly a woman of the west, of large spaces. You can imagine her holding the reins seated in a buckboard, or back another century, standing on the prow of a sailing ship, if women had been captains then. She reads her poems as if facing into a stiff breeze, her white hair back from her face, her cheeks rosy, her black eyes burning. She hooks audiences right away with her mix of righteous anger and humor.

Listing my chores for the day,
the decade, the next century, I note
that the planet needs saving –
by screaming, I suppose, out on
the street like a rabid banshee
hoisting a placard, shaking a fist,
when I'd rather ride by
in a carriage, smiling
and doing my queen wave

("Hard Times for Women")

Fionna is a feminist. She likes to remind young women that her mother and their grandmothers didn't have the vote, that we haven't come the whole way. In "Woodswoman" she remembers Judi Bari whose passionate defence of the old growth redwoods almost cost her life in a bombing and certainly contributed to her early death.

And absent now
the small hand
that beckoned us to risk
and fiddled a tune
to dance to
to sing with
to step out smartly by
on the way to jail
by way of the woods

to save trees
to save ourselves.

In another life, Fionna might have been a journalist with the world as her beat. For many years she worked at *The San Francisco News.* She missed being sent to the Pacific during World War II only because General MacArthur didn't want women journalists around. She's also an environmentalist who has walked the coastal forest with Sarah Flowers, neighbor, poet and California Park naturalist. Some years back, Fionna looked into the eyes of a wild bobcat who became a visitor in her house, even sat under her desk while she typed. In the course of his winter visit, the bobcat became her totem animal. In "Transmigration" she whispers to him,

While in the deep woods
I run at your side, keeping to shadows.
No eyes but yours
See the wildcat in womanskin.

At night, Fionna returns to her study to be alone and to write. Her social conscience, her community voice, is quieter in the late hours. Then the young girl of the mountains returns. The voice of the untamed spirit, a woman not easily resigned to limits nor to age comes forth. In "Eighty-Ton Mountain," Fionna is asked,

Aren't you about to be
eighty?
I who have been and intend
to stay five forever?
Yes, in August, I reply.
And the whole damn century
falls on me.

Though her poetry, fiction and essays have appeared in anthologies, periodicals, newspapers, this collection of poems is Fionna Perkins' first book. Putting together a lifetime of poetry wasn't easy. There was so much to consider, and looking back, Fionna, like most remarkable women, battled with self-doubt. She told me more than once that she felt her poetry was too plain beside more worldly, erudite writers. Her language, she feared, was not grand nor complex enough. What Fionna does is speak plainly. Her short lines sound simple, conversational, because she has pared them down to say exactly what she means about women, men and nature.

If ever a man did as he promised,
to cherish *the ground I walk on* – our
earth – *I'd never again stall his*
traffic and hear myself cursed.
I'd rather be home
in my garden, pruning
and pulling weeds.
("Hard Times for Women")
Barbara L. Baer

WHY PONIES?

When anyone asks, I say
they're ecological, keep the grass
down that with a spark in August
could set off a wildfire, then
convert the grass to fertilizer.
Birds dine off their leavings, nest
in the sheddings from their
winter coats. In the years of no
rain the ponies share alfalfa
with the deer, endure ravens as
chums every spring. I rationalize,
rarely tell the real why, the
songs the ponies sing to me waiting
for their grain, the bucking
bronco show they stage when let
out to pasture, the mad way
they run for love of running,
streaming through the trees, wind
visible. I say everything's
ecological, including laughter
and the lift to the heart.

SPACE TRAVEL

He told me once, driving
the edges of cliffs,
all sky above and below,
that every sound keeps moving out
further and further
forever.

Remembering now
the summer I was five
when my first whistle
broke through air as much miracle
as a space ship on Tranquility Bay,
I hear
from somewhere far past Jupiter
a faint piping.

LAKOTA LAND

Mountain born, I never understood
why my father loved the prairies.
He said at day's end he could look back
and see his tracks from the morning.
When I looked, I saw only a vast sky,
great reaches of unpeopled landscape.
Last night in a cafe on the Pacific shore
a gaunt troubadour in a cowboy hat
sang of Canada; he called his homeland
Big Lonely. In his melancholy tones
I heard the silence.

THE ITINERANT

Like the Scotch broom expanding
miles long, acres wide,
I am a transplant – from other
forests, higher mountains,
wheat fields, a desert, paths
on the journey to this land
of sandstone, these red trees,
a sky so often mist and at
its rim the vastest
of the many seas.

Here the piece of earth
I claim, knowing
my hold is temporal.

WITHIN THESE WALLS A POET

Squatting back from the street
with grass to walk across in front,
the fenced field beyond and once
nasturtiums wriggling under
the screen to cling flowering
against the door, this will always
be Myrna's house, where she
smoked and dreamed and wrote,
bringing the sea to her pen
in starlight and storm, where
gales raged in winter,
young redwoods grew tall
and the moon brought eerie shadows.
Here old sorrows
were remembered, the pastures
of youth made green again.

WINTER WITHOUT SONG

To lure a young and handsome
prince bewitched as frog, I built
a frog house my first summer
on the coast, layering sandstone
rocks at the edge of a garden pool,
leaving crevices
for him to hide in under water,
ledges for sunning and
catching flies.

He came at once, a princely
tree frog, and brought a tiny
mate, the two as green as our hills
in winter rains. He sunned, she
hid and together left as legacy
choruses to surround our house with
frog song when torrents
pool the drive with ponds.

Until this rainy winter night
when a radio voice gives ominous
news, *frogs disappearing everywhere,*
scientists baffled. Beside an open
window I listen chilled
to silence, aware I hear habitual
sounds from memory even absent,
hear now instead
a canary's dying notes.

MASKING THE REAL

Behind the bombast
and bluster
assertions of
done it
seen it
been there
frail mortal male flesh
a trembling tower
of uncertainties

RUNNING WILD

The men are running away again,
Going back to the woods, beating drums,
Beating their chests, howling like wolves,
Roaring like lions, chasing wildness,
Searching for fathers.

How far back? A road springs into vision,
Spinning away, spinning, spinning
Into distance,
Dipping, curving, rising beyond sight,
Past sheared green fields, fences, vineyards,
New orchards. How far?
The road speeds into land the color of dun,
Trod only by feet. Animal feet. How far?
Now, a darkening plain, a single tree. Africa.
A gray fog closing in as the road dissolves
In a blaze of midnight blue, then blackness,
The vision ends, saying how far.

The men are running away, lost sons.
Searching for fathers,
Running into the woods with tom-toms,
Shaking gourd rattles, wearing bearskins,
Teeth necklaces,
Making noises deep in their throats,
Deserting the totems of their phallic worship,
Projectiles aimed and fused,
Growing like wheat on the prairies,

Aloft in the heavens, flying like birds,
In the depths of oceans, swimming like fish,
Borne on the surface of seas
Like Jesus walking on water.

The men are running away backwards,
But the women are not following,
Not protesting. The women are praying
To Allah, to Jehovah, to the carpenter,
Mother Earth, the Great Spirit, the Marys,
To any deity or saint who will listen.
At desks and in their kitchens,
Leaning over cribs, computers, the weekly wash,
Singing in church, dancing without partners,
Paying bills, handing out change,
The women, seeing the exodus,
Are praying for the men to find fathers
Who saw a tree as phallic
And worshipped it.
Alive.

TRANSMIGRATIONS

You were a blue-eyed cat
with champagne hair who sang beneath
my window until I asked you in.
Guns boomed! You flew into the air
a bird and winged away to war,
vanished into space and stars,
leaving me infinity to wait.

Wars later, I let longing free
to drift in sky and wind.
You emerged on foot, eyes green
and clothed in fur, a tawny bobcat
stalking my woods and meadow,
sniffing at my doors. You risked death
a second time before I let you in.

Still warring, you were wounded.
Healed, you left again.
Now, the little house puss waits,
while in the deep woods,
I run at your side, keeping to shadows.
No eyes but yours
see the wildcat in womanskin.

AND WHAT IS HAPPENING WHERE YOU LIVE?

I bring you news from the country,
two shooting stars,
a Calypso orchid, armies
of Indian warriors,
headdresses feathered burgundy,
patches of sky splashed
on ceanothus, leathery-leafed
salal arrayed in ropes
of pink and white bells,
the huckleberry coral-tipped,
firs fluorescent.

A mateless peacock
on a neighbor's hill
screams these afternoons
and evenings,
'ELP! 'ELP!

Someone's scattered
handfuls of gold coins
into the duff under pines
violets and buttercups.

Seven flop-eared, knobbly-kneed Nubians
arrive all on the same day.
Two baby does seek homes where
they won't be eaten. Surely,
that silly old bird crying for company
knows the consequences
– more peacocks

HELP! HELP!

The news from the country
is rain.

HAIKU DIARY

in my California garden
a New England autumn
deck boards white with frost

I bask in winter sun
beyond the cliff edges
a sea of snow

maple branches
jeweled with silver pearls
the long rains

high on a green hill
spotted horses graze
on the fence a golden eagle

outside my window
a hum of bees
making apples

shed on bathroom tiles
the tail of a small dragon
cats stalking spring lizards

leaves of my life
falling in columns of figures
Ides of April

EPHEMERA

fog frames
a field in sun
I see a prairie landscape

soaring osprey call
my feet are earthbound

a lone leaf
flutters in the air
caught on a cobweb

WAITING OUT THE RAIN

Winter storms are winding down
the way our century is, not
all at once nor smoothly. I drive
from town through meres of
runoff, around wet curves into
spits of drizzle and up an incline
past leaning firs, exposed roots
about to lose their grip, as
I am, sloshing at the edge of
cabin-fever madness.

Five months of darkness
closed in with trees lashing
overhead, the yowl and whine of
gales battering the walls
and hearing an incessant drench
of rain falling on old soaked
deck boards, on windows, skylights,
roof shingles, squishy ground
and on my brain.

But where to run
screaming Mercy! Mercy!

In our woods pines snap and crash,
a cypress topples uprooted;
fleeing north I'd stall in the
Garcia's overflow, south to Jenner
the shelf is sliding to the sea,
and I remember childhood's
bone chill of blizzards.

Three feet of white ice
falling overnight
in the Sierra. On Mount Tam
winds peak at 127 miles
per hour. Do airplanes
fly in this?

To Mexico, to Rio,
to the South Seas? None
that I'd get on.

If rain stayed stacked
like snow, I'd be drowned
by now in over eighty inches.
Yet, today the sky's
almost back in place
and blue again. Tonight
the stars may shine.

SNOWBOUND

Her voice on a postcard, *When*
did life get so hard? Time, she is
talking about *time,* this teacher poet
I see stealing moments to pen a note,
still handwritten, still personal,
briefer now but always a reply.

Going breathless
through her days, there in
her handwriting, from reading to
writing to teaching and round
and round while in the country
without the teaching mine a
somewhat slower version.

Do we run each day in dread
of being crushed, as if a horde
is hot on our heels that we
must escape to survive, if barely,
only to hear on waking the pound
of pursuit in our temples?

As daily, hourly, by the seconds
a blizzard envelops us in what
we must know, must read, must
buy, must give to, must join, must
write in praise or protest of, a
bombardment by bevies of hucksters,
beggars, peddlers, wailers – all a
snow of paper muffling song.

Yet my friend's postcards
each time they come still sing.

AS THE CIRCLE EMPTIES

Still with me
through years of absence,
they appear unsummoned
to sit and visit
in rooms
they never knew.

I see their faces,
gestures, lips moving,
these interlopers
so casually at home
who make no sound.

The abiding grief,
they cannot hear
or speak aloud
nor can we ever
touch again.

KEEPSAKES

he stacks by the stove
for me to use as kindling
split sticks of precious wood

old redwood boards
from a fallen-in barn
silver on the outside

axed open to the
look and feel of satin
the color of cocoa

close but a shade all
its own growth years
mahogany streaks

he expects me to burn
these jewel-like remnants
of another age

redwoods no longer
left to grow to this
density this color

I set aside a few sticks
to bring out in secret
smile at stroke

marveling at simple beauty
eons of unmanaged growth
the blindness of men

FOR THE LOIS I WAS, THE FIONNA I AM

To tell the whole true story
of a pen name, I'd need
to write a book,
my family saga and his –
a name change I married ages
ago – bringing together
Vikings, Normans, Picts,
the Scots, some English, his
Indians and Welsh, a dash
of French, splits of German
both sides; this could grow
encyclopedic, simplest
way to explain,
I didn't like the name given,
chose my own.

TALKING WITH ADAM (WHO NEVER LISTENS)

Tracking my lineage, I retrace the trail to Eve and the rib story. I can't buy it, Adam. I prefer Lilith as model – your first wife, formed of dust from the four corners of earth, the same as you, Adam, who tore around the planet as your equal and with a temper to match. You clashed, of course, she wanting a dyarchy and you determined to be the first man a king.

Who arranged the divorce? God? I doubt it. He'd just invented birds, and their antics fascinated him. More likely the work of hired scribes rewriting his and her stories, demoting women healers to chambermaids and relegating Lilith to myth and prehistory.

Still, there's no war between us, Adam, except as you make one by turning hostile and combative when I decline to play the roles you choose for me, of underling, of indulgent mother, of fantasy heart-of-gold whore or of victim like poor hapless used and misused Eve.

How you see the rest of us – hoo, boy! What a crew of monsters!

Witches, sirens and snake-headed demons souring cow pastures, singing sailors to death in inlets of rock and mysteriously draining you and your brethren of vital fluids in the night, and werewolfesses, vampiresses, stalking cats any size anywhere, chimeras, gargoyles and whatever weird being recurs in your worst nightmares – *these are ME?*

If strong or kindly, Adam, you think me odd – *different.* Fierce and protective, a maniac. Perceptive and intelligent, I'm – God forbid – competing! Sensitive, over-emotional, intuitive, practicing the black arts; expressing empathy, mawkish or maudlin.

Wise? – ah, there's the crone – beware the evil she may spread abroad with spells and secret midnight stews of *Amanita pantherina,* newt eyes, grizzly claws and tansy leaves.

So we're back to Eve, whose name in Hebrew means life. What exactly was her sin? She was hungry and ate a prize apple being saved for the county fair? You would know, Adam, if she were already pregnant with Cain. *I'm starving,* she'd say and wanting your get to endure.

Wasn't that what God intended?

PASSING THE TORCH

Months I ran in skirts to his
bellowed BOY! a wartime replacement
for the young male copy runners
drafted for the killing shores, the
deadly skies, the engulfing seas.
The day he called to me by name
I had earned a desk, a typewriter,
a niche to say was mine.

His the kingdom of illusion, to
write for others whether well
or poorly done, who once had played
the knights and knaves of Elizabethan
times, bounding onto stages to give
wings to Shakespeare's lines, this
man had grown so hugely fat his
stomach sagged to chair seat, and I
had been his legs, fetching papers,
paste pots, clippings from the morgue,
handfuls of pencils sharpened daily,
gallons of coffee by the cup.

I stood before him naked clothed,
seeing spread open on his desk
the day's edition, his finger jabbing
at a bylined story – mine – 35my first
and his the verdict dreaded most.
It came heavy as a judge's sentence,
I'd like to lock YOU in a room with
nothing but a typewriter. Telling me
I was good, I had the makings, I
could go places. Trained from infancy
against the risk of being vain to
never quite hear praise, I stammered,
blushed fiery and fled.

All ancient history now, forgotten,
of another time, another place,
but I did hear. I have remembered.
He's still there at his desk a half
century ago, scowling up at me,
daring me. I was young then,
and Claude's long dead.

FIRST DATE

Rather than finding a name for the small
tea bowls we held in circled thumbs
and forefingers, kept refilling,
I discover trained monkeys in *The*
Thousand Recipe Chinese Cookbook
scaling the highest peaks in all
China to pick tea leaves growing
closest to the gods, dried, infused
and sipped later as *Cloud Mist* or
to credit the workers *Monkey Pluck.*

Another instance of how often I start
in one direction, end somewhere
else, like buying the cookbook at a
kitchen-store closing when I went there
for pasta bowls and a new spatula
or being long rooted into the North
Coast when my dream was to travel
the world beginning with China.

Instead I agreed to a date with the
young sailor who claims I was two hours
late, while I admit to one, remembering
he out-waited me and wasn't supposed to
so here we are fifty-four years later
still sitting across a round table
from each other as we did in a curtained
booth upstairs on Grant Avenue.

When the Chinese waiter brought menus,
a pot of tea and the two little bowls
the young man looked as if about to
be crucified or now that I know the look
poisoned by the first Chinese meal of
his life, owned up to years after.
We didn't ask the name of the tea, must
have been *Eyebrows of Longevity.*

READ ALMOST ALL ABOUT IT

Fish wrappers, we said with a shrug,
disparaging the pages we wrote,
knowing ours were throw-away words,
fire-starters, liners for bottoms
of bird cages, the columns of daily
news ephemeral, repetitious as
breathing – who was born, who died,
who currently was killing whom,
who had won or lost, was wedded
divorced crowned deposed elected
defeated and on and on. Year
after year names dates ages, the
who-what-when-where but rarely
the why or sketchily, deadlines
relentless, space needed for ads,
neither the time nor demand for
anonymous scribes to dig that deep.

HISTORY LESSON

Since our morning's wrong turn, having
to circle back and start over, I feel
on a treadmill, moving but standing still,
a mile backward for every mile ahead,
at Port Gamble stepping out into more than
a century in reverse, a lumber mill's
company town, ghosts thick and pressing in.

We've come to this spot of preserved
timbering history as a kind of
pilgrimage, earn our livelihood using
what's made from cutting trees –
paper. The connection once much closer,
my father with bandaged head home from
the woods, had the axe cut deeper, I'd
have been left at six half-orphan.

Here I find no memorials to logging
mishaps, no historic markers to record
men and their families having to pack up
and move on over the next hill, to the
next town, the next state when the show's
over, the woods played out. Nor are
any souls owed to the company store
tacked up to the walls like trophies.

None of that hard scrabble life shows in
these quiet swept streets, in the
beautifully reproduced New England church,
the clean silent corridors of the old
company office building, the old post
office, the superintendent's grand house
overlooking the mill, now even the store
itself mostly museum and seashells.

Yet down on the flat where Hood Canal
joins the sound, a mill still operates
that sawed its first big trees into
planks for mill walls the autumn of
1853, the trees that grew then so
huge and thick a man could scarcely
walk among them, hemlock, grand fir,
Douglas fir, Sitka spruce, red cedar,
seedlings in the Sixth and Seventh
Centuries – the company's first cut.

The ghosts I brought walk with us as we
look around, read the markers, visit the
cemetery – my rancher father in Montana
who turned horse logger early years of
the century before *Cats* replaced horses,
late Thirties his son a *Cat doctor*
at a logging camp out of Alturas before
chain saws replaced axes and crosscuts,
what would they say of chip mills, feller
bunchers, timber harvest plans book
lengths long, a half dozen camouflage terms
for clear cuts and industry talk of
regrowing Western ridges and canyons
like flatland fields of corn.

As we drive away again past the pyramid
of wood chips, alders, a clear cut, we
see in the new forest of spindly young
firs a sign announcing the company's in
its *Third Harvest Cycle,* its final cut
chipping trees for pulp – twelve centuries
of forest growth gone in less than two.

WOODSWOMAN

beware
when women
go into big timber
to hug trees
to stand between trees
and catskinners
feller-bunchers
D-sixes

using
their bodies
as message
their lives
as warning

big trees out there
big saws
big angry men

and absent now
the small hand
that beckoned us to risk
and fiddled a tune
to dance to
to sing with
to step out smartly by
on the way to jail
by way of the woods

to save trees
to save ourselves

HARD TIMES FOR WOMEN

Listing my chores for the day,
the decade, the next century, I note
that the planet needs saving – by
screaming, I suppose, out on
the street like a rabid banshee,
hoisting a placard, shaking a fist,
          when I'd rather ride by
          in a carriage, smiling
          and doing my queen wave.

I hate being jostled by bodies,
roared at, hassled, arrested,
going limp in debris – a disgrace
to my mother, a public nuisance
          – how often
          I'm told, and
          at times I agree.

If ever a man did as he promised,
to *cherish* the ground I walk on – *our*
earth – I'd never again stall his
traffic and hear myself cursed.
          I'd rather be home
          in my garden, pruning
          and pulling weeds.

Yet it's still the same as always,
whether wanting the vote or saving the
world, stopping a war, needing a pay
raise or care for the children,
          out in the street
          with my banners and bitches
          marching and going to jail.

COAST COUNTRY YEAR

the wind mourns
trees droop, weeping
on deserted shores

mounds of snow
dot rain-soaked pastures
newborn lambs

at road's edge
a nosegay of poppies
the bulldozer missed

on the dunes
a sea of lavender
waves of lupine

nesting season
ravens harry
a lone hawk

bells peal
a carillon in the tree top
thrush greets the sun

gray boulders
moving in the meadow
a burst upward – quail

the cove vanishes
into night and fog
a scarlet afterglow

on August gales
a keening cry
osprey soaring

blue beads
unstrung into a pail
huckleberry pie

translucent coral
sun through fan of feathers
Red-tailed hawk

shadows gliding
in a sunset sky
night birds

walks carpeted
with bronze and gold
a year falling

storm raging
old cat lies dying
heart young as spring

coast Christmas
red berries, green pines
mud

T.S. YOU WERE RIGHT ON

How do the wind gods know
it's All Fools' Day?
First day of April every year
the wind from the west
cuts across the green pastures,
knifes through the trees,
flattening flower beds and
scattering apple blossoms
in showers of unmelting snow
where it never snows.
April, you are *the cruellest month.*
Your winds sandpaper my soul.

STONE WOMAN

I cry out of dark caverns
scarred invisible
    an unfruiting leaf
    the seedless bloom

JUST IMAGINE

you're coming up
from your basement shaky
in the eerie stillness
after a horrendous blast
must have blown
the world to bits knees
water ears pounding
you want a hot cup of tea
or a big gulp of your
medicinal brandy if you
didn't drink it all those
frigid days of last winter
but at the top of the stairs
there's nothing
no hallway to the kitchen
no kitchen

should you go back down
and try again you may be
hallucinating it was the noise
did something to your head
you take another step
find your foot on bare ground
swept clean
by a giant broom

your whole house
is gone and the houses
across and down the street
there isn't even a street
you look up and around

as if expecting the kindling
that was your home
to rain down and reassemble itself
like building a house
on a computer

all you have left
is yourself standing roofless
in your old gray sweater
a faded T-shirt worn sandals
and baggy pants some
junk and old stuff stored
in the basement a little
money in the bank if
there still is a bank
but without an I.D. or a
deposit book how can you prove
it is yours

you missed your moment for
screaming tears burned
dry from shock if you keep
standing in this spot you'll
turn to stone so you
pick up a foot that is
deadweight and put it in front
of the other remember from
the calendar in your kitchen
that the month is April
and start walking into spring
while it's still daylight

DROUGHT

A century without rain
– no, 125 years
since California
was so dry – it's all those
new people bathing,
washing their cars
and wanting prime timber
from the watersheds
for 125 years.

Meanwhile, the pines are dying,
dwarf mistletoe
eating to the crowns
and seeding for the August shoot-out
– they learned artillery
or taught us – at sixty miles per hour,
and the hot dry winds
will carry death
to wherever pines are green.

ON THE BRINK

Scraped redwood ridges
north slopes bare
of Douglas fir
madrone chinquapin and tan oak
chipped for pressboard
only twigs and leaves
crushed huckleberry
and saplings left to hold
stump deserts

while down the last incline
where waves wash
a continent's evergreens
stop growing

are forests ever listed
as endangered
the planet's lungs
oxygen for mine

WRAITHS AND ROAMERS

Have you come again, my old
lost love in the guise of a wilding?
Twenty years since I last watched
the bobcat swing away around
the corner of our house
            leaving my world
            going back into his.

What is the life span of
Lynx rufus, eight years, ten?
He should be long dead in his
last incarnation. The creature
now prowling the perimeters
of sight his get, three
generations down?

Behaving as the bobcat did
all the months of a summer, the
fall, a wet winter, appearing,
disappearing, then gone for good
like certain men of my life.

Not one I could ever set a clock
by to tell how long he'd be away or
when he might return. With the
bobcat, his forest was logged.
There was drought. With men, the
wars and depressions, maybe
boom times even worse.

Twice this one has been sighted,
bolting for cover under the deck,
streaking away over the garden
walk, now crashing into brush
up behind the house
            moving like wind
            like lightning
            like a bobcat.

Ponies swerve to face the spot,
ears pricked. They know wild.
I see the flash of a furred
body the color of a deer but
small as a new fawn, legs
stretched up as if to
snag a tree hold.

In sudden silence I walk up
to look, see only salal, bracken,
pine cones, young redwood, no broken
branches, no indentations in the
duff, hear no crackling of needles
underfoot. This wilding, too,
has vanished without a sound like
an old lost love leaving
his shape-changing ghost behind.

WINGING HOME

Of cones collected and saved the
three I'll remember – a ponderosa from
the Sierra, a sugar pine from high
in the coastal mountains and off
our own land a Douglas fir named for
David the Scot who walked Pacific
rain forests barefoot over a century
ago gathering seeds and specimens,
died of the rigors soon after.

They lay atop a bookshelf
season after season, mementos
collecting dust, until the
season of release arrives, seeds
suddenly everywhere about the
room, lighting on surfaces
where no tree will ever grow.

I gather by fingertip specks
of tissue paper, filmy wings
the reddish color of bark
on the inside and with hand cupped
carry them outdoors, uncurl my
fingers into gusts of air,
see them drift away, and I
smile, planting a forest.

CHOICE

For him an easy death,
legs buckling, body going limp
an instant after the injection,
weeks of indecision ended.

When is the moment
to ask the mercy killing
for an old and faithful friend,
when he whimpers,
tries to rise and legs collapse?

I said *It's time.*
But how could I be sure?
His own one life, like ours,
was all he had. In pain,
failing, did he want
another hour, another day?

Vacillating, I read of a
doomed baby that doctors could
have kept alive more days, even
weeks. The parents chose to let
her go, together holding their
joined lives her last hours.

Whether an old dog, new life
forming, a fatally impaired infant,
saying yes to death
claims two, the one that goes,
the one that stays.

We keep private anniversaries,
we women. Signing the paper,
I died a little, die
again at each remembering.

SUMMER COLLAGE

for Lucie

a snow-sheathed mountain
memory of winter cold
icy nights
black and white of an old artist
who painted flowers
and said of friendship
takes time
how long ago ours began
an August evening
Ruth's birthday
my birthday
yours just past
six of us then
the porch wound in wisteria
warmth of the day lingering
in the soft stillness
faces turn seaward
as night comes down

WILD MUSTARD

Wild mustard winds north
a Spanish trail to home
– conquistadors long gone

hills on hills
shimmer under August light
California gold

SEPTEMBER PALETTE

Stark and lonely
the leaning sheds
moss-edged fences
here in the roll of hills
at first rain so quickly green
as soon gone to gold

and there
the wide, wide sea
curtained in mists
that hang like still smoke
over treetops and ridges

gray, green and gold
the colors of home ground

SMALL SONGS TO AUTUMN

dangling at the fuchsias
Monarchs sup
the last of summer's sweetness

above the quiet graves
massed choirs of pink angels
fall's naked ladies

October air
a crisp gold apple
the first bite

music in the woods
startled quail lift off
with a thrum-m-m

trails of fog
trees vanish into gray
the lonely time

THE HORSE ORCHARD

for Malcolm

THE HORSE ORCHARD

Storm

Above us at three in the morning the sky
    stretched from low ridge to sea line
as big as Montana's, stars we marveled at,
    that long since we'd last seen a night
sky so brilliant, trees too small to
    intrude their dark shapes against that
vast dome, while down from an unfinished
    house rolled dunes of sandy soil bulldozed
bare except for three minute redwood groves,
    two wild rhododendrons and a fir sapling
no taller than I – thirty years from then
    until now in this wilderness of sand, sea
and trees to come to this, standing out in
    the open, pines all around, water streaming
off hair, face, fingertips, water drenching
    an old pony, as far as he would be led.

Not colic, walking him will do no good,
    he is shivering, breathing hard –
is this the day, *his time?* I saw it
    last spring when the ravens plucked
the short side of his mane bare, exposed
    a skeletal look to his frame. My throat
tightened on tears. I did not weep.

Why do the ravens rebuild
every year –
they never leave?

Here where rain falls like a fusillade,
    where water lies on saturated slopes
waiting its turn for a run to the sea,
    pines have stood eaten by parasites
for so long they snap in hurricane gales,
    take others down. Here in the dead
and quiet of winter with the month, the
    year nearly at an end, our woods are
a howling maelstrom of lashing trees,
    roaring canyons of creeks become cascades,
everything in turbulence, in cacophony
    except in one spot where an old pony
has decided to make a last stand.

No tears, not yet,
only the sky weeps.

The relentless, unsparing torrent pours
    over him, his thick winter coat sodden,
his locked hind feet water-logged. I hold
    warm bran to his mouth, and he gives me
his big-eyed dark look, draws in a bare
    mouthful, other times as craving of bran
as he is of apples. I wipe him down rubbing
    rubbing, trying to warm his heart,
bloodstream, lungs and adamant brain. I think
    of the story my brother told, of Mama
flapping her apron at a cow down in the snow.

Flapping her apron, pulling
its tail to get the cow on its feet
to keep it from freezing.

I'm supposed to move
beyond my mother – does it count
as a plus that I'm farther
south and west, in a rainstorm
rather than a blizzard, cook
with electricity instead of wood?
Still treasured, her cast iron
Dutch oven, bequeathed to me
with a crack in the lid.

We cover this old pony with a dry blanket,
    soggy in minutes. We need the rain to stop,
we need sun, a heated barn without leaks,
    piles of warm dry towels to rub away
his chill, the magic carpet to transport
    him. We need a horse vet, the closest
fifty miles north, eighty miles east.

The little left of the day
darkens to night. Would a vet
even drive the coast road
for any amount of money – his
trip perhaps in vain? I know what
I don't want to know, as I
have known so much about this
pony from his first day.

The wet on my cheeks
is rain
not tears.

For twenty-two years he's been my pony, oh,
    longer – twenty-two and a half. Brought here
mid-June, he bolted at first sight of me.
    Horse strategy – outrun the enemy, this
strange woman, this strange new place. Except
    that he was staked, hooked to a chain,
the chain to a peg in the ground. He ran out
    to the end and endlessly in circles,
while I stood unmoving, saying soft and low,
    You're all right, you're all right – easy,
easy, I won't hurt you. Saying it over and
    over and waiting – waiting until he understood
I meant him no harm. When finally he stopped
    and just stood, we looked at each other.

I laughed, went to him
and stroked his neck. The knowing
of each other, the bonding began – the
Scotch of us.

This pony and I have looked at each other
    our stubborn times, will against will,
as my father and I looked at each other,
    measuring how far to push, how long
to resist. We're into one of those
    now – he's not budging.

Black as moonless midnight the day
    he came, mane cropped, the only white
at ankle and coronet above his two back
    hooves, and freshly scarred. He had
broken out onto a road and been hit by a
    truck, a truckload of men to hold
him down for his deep wound to be dressed.

Scar still shows, coat gone rusty and shot
   with gray, a spreading patch of snow on
his forehead, mane black as ever and never
   cut, falls loose like an Indian pony's.

Mated and with the two he sired,
he brought his family to the house
Christmas Eve, all looking like
shaggy, big-eyed bears, winter coats
dry and bushed out on a day of no
rain. We fed them apples and sang
carols. They listened politely.

They are a family, the four ponies.
   When I found him in distress and snapped
on the lead, the other three ran in and
   around, bucking and kicking to break
him free, to challenge him to run. Did they
   sense it is his time, that I'm taking
him away? Again I am his enemy?

But it comes to this,
he is old.

Their last race, once always out in front, black
   mane and tail streaming, he stayed off
to the side, not joining their play – the
   kicking, the bucking, the dead-heat gallop –
despite all their efforts to entice him.
   Seeing him there alone, just watching, I
didn't laugh or clap for their performance.

I wanted to cry,
his time closer than I thought.

Years before our destinies merged, I saw him
    on the highway, one of an odd little
procession, a goat, a donkey and a black pony
    strung out alongside and following a
big white horse. Christmastime. I fanced them
    a caravan on a pilgrimage to Bethlehem.
More likely, one had found an open gate or a
    broken fence, and they were off to see the
world, unherded, unhitched, unsaddled, unpacked,
    unguarded, having themselves a time.

From tracking this pony
to bring him home, we learned
it's horse nature to go walkabout
in his own pasture, at the neighbor's
or off in the hills, if he's a stallion
and mare musk is on the wind.

He may not have been the horse I would have
    chosen. He was the horse that came for the
one I'd wanted since the ranch in Montana, taken
    there an infant by team and wagon from Kalispell
some sixty miles away, through Marion and Pleasant
    Valley, up in the northwest corner where trees
grow – or did. My brother's last visit, he found
    the old ranchland and homestead clear cut.

Grandpa had sold
timber rights even before
we left, broke.

We and our families, this pony and I, have known
    some hard times through the centuries. He's
well-proportioned but small, ten hands, a Shetland,
    his recent forebears stunted by the harsh climate
and scant forage on the rocky isles north of the
    Highlands from which half of my forebears took
ship for Canada to be free of the English invaders.

Shetlands, a little Scot
from Aberdeen told me, were used
in the mines – *pit ponies* – and when
they came up, he said, they were
blind. He had seen them running on
the moors, herds of three and
four hundred in times past.

Does this old pony intend to stand here
as if abandoned by God till he
falls down dead to prove it?
I won't have it, not this time.

To keep him company and to keep him home, we took
    on a welfare case, a little chestnut Welsh
mare with a white blaze, a neck infection, a
    misshapen face from an undersized halter
and a creak when she walked. He would have come
    from the ends of the earth to claim her.

Catching her scent, he raced across the
    clearings, halted on a knoll where she
could see him, head up, neck arched, tail
    lifted in a plume, and trumpeted his pent-up
longing, his adoration – two foals later gelded.

His beautiful bugling
forever silenced.

The herd father still,
leading his family off all around
the neighborhood till one
Last Great Roundup when
we had to fence him, his family
and us in – how I hated it,
the fences.

A legacy of the cattle ranch and homestead at
the end of the wagon ride from Kalispell, first
horse years for me, the last for the
rest of the family, ending with a horse and sleigh
ride just before Christmas to Jennings, a name gone
from the maps, there till August and moving
again, the day of my fourth birthday, the family
leaving for good, leaving Montana and taking it
with them in stories and memories and pictures.

I with scant memory
of my birthplace grew up
with theirs, Montana as
wild and free and unfenced,
of lakes and evergreens, the
mountains and meadows and
plains, of beautiful horses
and a sky as big as the world,
with Montana as Eden,
Montana as myth.

Near this open drenching spot a woodland bower
ringed by young redwoods and two tall old
pines, the branches offering some shelter from
the rain that keeps pounding down, a bed of
needles a foot or two deep. He likes being in
the trees, has his favorite groves. The barn's
too far, no doors to keep him in. We can try
what we do when he has colic – pull and push.

Drag and shove – once kept him up
and walking six hours when
all he wanted to do was lie down
and roll himself to death.
He'd eaten the potato vines,
should have killed him,
wasn't his time.

We move him an inch or two,
a few more, a foot,
give him a rest and try again.

At the opening he steps in on his own. His way,
    just don't hurry or push him, he'll get around
to it in his time, to stand for the currying, the
    shots, the hoof trimming. I tie him against
the chance of his going out in the open to stand.
    We exchange wet blanket for a dry one, put dry
hay around and under. We look at each other. It's
    okay. He may squeak through this one, too.

Suddenly we are pelted with hail.
Dare I curse the gods
when last fall was the start
of the seventh year of drought?
Each day harder to say we
need the rain, tonight impossible.

I swipe at my cheeks, wet with rain,
melting hail, tears – hope fading.

We go inside for coffee, weather report warns
    of hazardous road conditions, don't even
think of calling the vet. *Should we call a*
    neighbor to bring a gun and put him down,
the man asks. I shake my head. How do I
    explain my knowing from all the deaths I've
sat or stood with, that he's not really suffering?

He's just dying.
It takes a while,
like getting born.

While God may have abandoned this old pony to
the furies of a coast winter, I have not.
He shall have his time to do this his way, in
whatever quiet and peace the storm will allow
and with what dignity and grace he can muster.
A horse for all his services to man's family
through the ages and to me in my lifetime
is due that.

When I go back out,
he is down.

Brothers

Twice my brother told me the story of the wild
stallion he longed to have as his own, big and
rangy, a dark bay with black mane and tail.
He had seen it on one of his rides with our
older brother, dead now many years. No more than
eight or nine then, he is the only one left
to tell the stories of how they saddled up early
in the morning, the two boys on a ranch the
hell and gone from Kalispell and rode off into the
hills, young *caballeros* on the hunt for a herd
of wild horses to chase or join.

Gone all day, he said,
no one knew where, nobody
ever worried.

How would a boy know, not there to see her
go to the door, look out to the hills and
across the meadows and pastures, eyes alert for
distant movement, the sight of a horse, a
boy's blonde head or a dark one? My mother too,
she worried but kept it to herself.

In her wilderness of below-zero winters, of summer
    forest fires, where she pumped water from a well,
washed clothes by hand, baked bread in a wood range,
    alone with children in a woods of ponderosa and
lodgepole pine, of larch and fir and aspen, willows
    bordering Little Wolf Creek, Indians camped
nearby in hunting season, squaws coming to sit in
    her kitchen and watch her cook, had she her
prayers and rituals, as I have mine?

Faith, I mutter, *have faith.*
I ask God for strength,
little else. I need faith that
somehow I can muddle through.
But to where
and for what purpose?

We had covered all but the pony's head with the
    bright blue tarp to keep him as warm and dry
as possible, barely possible under the dripping
    branches on his mat of damp needles in the
rain the rain the rain that falls without let-up,
    without mercy. He lies quiet, no thrashing or
heaving or gasping for more air, more life.

He has walked this earth
as far as he's going – his decision,
and I have acquiesced, cannot stop
the rain nor bring out the sun, there'll
be no heroic, life-saving gestures.

Like us, he too has lived thirty years at the edge
    of the sea, through summers of no grass, searing
heat, abrasive winds and plagues of flies, winters
    with trees crashing in his corral, ground turned
to mush, ice in his water and in any season the
    gray weeks of stagnant fog that chills and smothers.
Two droughts in his lifetime. Old bodies weary with
    the effort to brace and stand against the extremes.

My old pony's soft
green days had become
fewer and farther between.

My brother said I was the dreamer, yet surely the
boy he once was dreamed of riding the wild
stallion, the big dark bay with black mane and
tail, trailed by a colt the same color. Like
Pegasus, he would carry my brother light as air
over mountains and rivers, across canyons.

And out to the ends of the world
for the boy to see
what was there.

Then a mare of ours whose scent drew the stallion? My
father, the man in the Stetson, cocked and worn
low on his forehead, his two sons and Cousin Alec
corralled him. A few ecstatic moments he was my
brother's as the boy watched the great beautiful wild
bay thunder once around the corral, leap the
fence and knock off the top rail. His colt followed,
was over and gone, neither ever seen again.

On my brother's face, in his eyes,
as he told the story, I saw
his dream horse seventy years later
still sailing over a fence,
Pegasus flying back to freedom.

Wake

Near midnight, his breathing barely audible, the man,
the dog and I with him, waiting. Waiting inside,
only a matter of time, waiting through and for it to
end. For the man an eternity.

For me clocks had stopped moving
at finding my old pony shivering and wheezing. I
kneel by his head in the beam of a flashlight in the
man's hand, see and hear his intake of one longer,
deeper breath like a sigh at the end of a long walk.
My vision blurs. I undo his halter.

His head falls away
from my hand,
he is gone.

No longer an improbable hope to cling to.
I could weep and couldn't although later
inside I would groan and cry out, *It hurts!*
It hurts! To the Scotch of me it would
be unseemly to fling myself across his body,
sobbing. Yet he has been my friend and
companion through years of lonely days.

My old pony's dignity
and reserve facing his own
death, can I match it,
losing him?

There would be no new pony here ever to
wear his halter. I lift it off and
rub the white patch on his forehead
for the last time. He was unshackled
now to run wild and free through the
pastures of heaven.

Again, a young stallion,
black as moonless midnights,
running with all the beautiful
mares, and no one ever
to come with halter and lead
to take him back to
limited range or fences.

The blue tarp now a shroud, beneath its stiff
    plastic folds all that remains of the little
black horse that I have grown a pasture for,
    have fed, combed and brushed, talked to and
sung to, have chased after, been dragged by,
    have cursed, whacked and walked to keep him
alive till I was ready to drop and once faced
    giving the word to put him down when he
foundered and couldn't walk.

He was my past and a place I barely remember,
    he was the brothers and the man in the
Stetson, he was the Montana of myth, Montana
    as Eden – a pony I loved beyond reason.

All this gone from my life
between one morning
and the next.

We walk out from under
the dripping branches, the man,
the dog and I, into a drizzle,
into the dark, into almost
midnight and a new day, as the
month, the year and the century wanes.

Where did Christmas go and
take its songs of hope in the dark
and dead of winter? My old pony's
serenade, as soft to the ear
as velvet to the touch, I have
heard for the last time.

Were I now to weep, I might
flood the world.

In the night, dry-eyed and unsleeping, hour
    after hour, I hear the steady fall of rain,
see the pony's body there under the blue
    tarp, his death all the deaths, and I relive
each one, a night as unending as when my father
    died, he dies again, and it is agony, the
pain in my gut, the salt sting of unshed tears.
    I am a lake, a river, an ocean of tears
dammed to bursting, and I cannot cry.

First thing next morning
we let her out of the corral, his
mate with the honey mane and white blaze.
She streaks across the pastures
to where his body is – how does she
know? – young mare and gelding follow
more slowly, shy from me who took
him away, mare sniffs at an exposed
hoof, young one paws at the blue
tarp, demanding he get up, they form
a half circle and just stand,
silent, heads lowered.

Burial

A machine is coming to dig
the grave, and the mare still
keeps her vigil. We take the leads
and walk the three back
to the corral.

Today the burying. A dead horse soon stinks
    and to high heaven. In Depression years in
Oregon outside the mill town where we lived, an
    old horse died along our road, got that far,
and he'd had enough. Like the men riding in on
    the rails from all over the country, he
didn't belong to anyone there, and nobody knew
    where he'd come from. His decay made our air
putrid for days. It saddened me then and still,
    that old derelict horse stumbling along
until he fell, and no one cared, and who
    knew how many of the men likewise?

The storm has subsided to give us
a dry day but there's little grace or dignity in
burying a pony by backhoe. No flowers,
bushes bird-stripped of berries, I
toss in branches of redwood and pine,
the trees that sheltered him his last hours.
We pay the man and thank him for coming
so quickly when needed. He tells us
he nearly died of cancer a short
while ago – fine now.

The coast full of us who squeak
through time after time
but not always.

A life never before on this earth that is
    never to be again has just perished.
My old pony, like snowflakes, like me, was
    a species of one. If his two foals die
unbred, his line that somehow goes back
    forty million years to *Eohippus* will
vanish, as will our two lines – the man's and
    mine – that joined this century, when
childless we meet our time. Three-and-a-half
    million years in the making of us.

Someone should take note
of these untabulated,
unremarked extinctions.

New Year's Eve we celebrate
the passing of time at the hotel
that has stood in one spot
most of the century.
I dance with a young plumber,
both of us doing a kind of logger's
stomp on the bare redwood floor,
stomping out the pain and
grief, the losses and defeats of the
year gone, stomping in victory
at making it through and stomping
a bittersweet joy at having the chance at
another spin of the wheel.

I've come to know
what the stomping's all about.
He may, too, in time.

Walking the land alone at dusk
a day later I see everywhere I look the
black form and fall of mane of a
horse grazing that I can run up to, run
my hand through into air, know
finally that he is gone.

I cannot bear that I shall never
see my pony again,
and I bear it.

New Century

A page of the calender turned,
behind us seven years since
that night, the two tall pines older
and shaggier and the sapling
redwoods taller and thicker – the trees
of the bower that sheltered
a small dying horse. The other ponies
never go there, I keep it clear
of fallen branches should deer
ever choose to bed in that spot. Where
his head lay, a tan oak has sprouted,
now nearly two feet tall,
the perfect tribute.

No ordinary time or small storm
could have brought him down. His was
not the falling of a leaf nor even
of the tree itself crashing to
the ground or felled.

He was the whole orchard – a world
vanishing or already gone.

WELCOME BACK

A lone and lonesome voice
calls up to me
with the sound of an ancient gate creaking open
its rusty hinges a rasp
a voice that needs companions
the chorister mourning for
his vanished choir
unmistakably a
croak *a frog's croak* –
my bewitched prince home
after so long absent
and if I could catch him
now tonight in the rain-soaked
fern and periwinkle
somehow hold him from
leaping seven leagues away
I'd hug him to death
that glad to know he's
still alive

EIGHTY-TON MOUNTAIN

My ingenuous poet friend
for whom nothing is taboo
everything a curiosity
to be lifted and looked under
and around and dug up
for stray diamonds
asks without warning,
Aren't you about to be
eighty?
I who have been and intend
to stay five forever?
Yes, in August, I reply.
And the whole damn century
falls on me
the mountain of years
already climbed
ahead only a slide downhill
and over the edge.
Flattened, I hear, *Whoa, girl*
– my father's voice – *get up*
and stop crying. And I see
my mother keep walking the time
the snake slithered
into her path, and he
moved out of the way,
she didn't.
Dawn the day of my birth
I'm up and trudging along
as she did
face forward
into the territory ahead.

ALERT!

Twice at early light
a raven flew by my window,
raucous cries jolting

me awake to fears of
omens and sudden demise,
though hardly premature,

given that I was here
for the third decade of a
century now in its ninth,

affording me a great span
of miraculous and traumatic
years to contemplate,

if focused backward, having
lived them, but to look ahead
it seems no time at all,

as if I've just stepped off
an airplane or down from a bus,
my bags still packed.

BEAR IT ALL AWAY

From high above treetops
comes the piercing cry,
that lost weeping voice – a mother
searching for a child, the wait
for the lover who never comes, hands
tearing at shards of a shattered house
– again again the plaintive notes,
there in the twilight sky a bird
keens for all our sorrows.
How late the fisher hawk
flies home.

ACKNOWLEDGEMENTS

My thanks to the editors of the following magazines and books in which some of these poems, sometimes in slightly different form, have previously been printed.

American Poetry Anthology, "Space Travel"

Arts & Entertainment Magazine, "Small Songs to Autumn"; "T.S., You Were Right On"; "Passing the Torch"

At Our Core, Papier-Maché Press, "Hard Times for Women"

Cartwheels on the Faultline, Floreant Press, "Talking With Adam (Who Never Listens)"

Coast Magazine, "Drought"

Convolvulus #11, "Winter Without Song"; "*#14*, "Read Almost All About It"

Colored Horse Studios Broadside, "Hard Times for Women"

GAB, "Within These Walls A Poet"; "September Palette"; "The Itinerant"

Haight Ashbury Literary Journal, "Lakota Land"; "Transmigrations"

Outlook, "Wraiths and Roamers"

Rainy Day Women Press, "Transmigrations"

Ridge Review, "Running Wild"; "Lakota Land"

Saltwater, Sweetwater. Women Write from California's North Coast, Floreant Press, "And What is Happening Where You Live?"; "Woodswoman"

Sojourn, "Snowbound"

Steelhead Special Issue #18, "Winging Home"; *Special Issue #19,* "Bear It All Away"

The Land of Six Seasons, "Coast Country Year"

The Redwood Coast Review, "First Date"

The Thousand Recipe Chinese Cookbook, ©1988 Gloria Bley Miller. Information on Chinese teas in "First Date"

Third Thursday Poets, "Haiku Diary" (published as "At Summer's End"); "Summer Collage"; "Within These Walls a Poet"

This Far Together: Haight Ashbury Literary Journal Anthology 1980-1995, "Transmigrations"

Women Talking, Women Listening, "Stone Woman"

Wood, Water, Air and Fire: The Anthology of Mendocino Women Poets, "As the Circle Empties"; "Choice"; "Alert"

Word Weavers, "Haiku" (published as "Coast Highway"); "Mendocino Summer"; "Ephemera"; "Why Ponies?"

And my gratitude to all who have aided and encouraged me through the years.

Floreant Press would like to thank Dee Watt for reading and selection, as well as Lucie Marshall and Marilyn Kinghorn for proofreading.

Photo: David Torres

Born August 13, 1919, in Kalispell, Montana, named Lois Jacqueline Sinclair, fourth and last child of Norman and Ethel Sinclair. The family gave up ranching in Montana in the early twenties, moved first to Idaho, then Washington, settling in Oregon. Attended a dozen schools in four states. First poetry published in *The Gatherer,* winter of 1936, in San Francisco. Worked for *The San Francisco News* during and after World War II, eleven years a reporter with the byline: Lois Thomas. In 1960, started the first bookstore in Mendocino Village, and moved to the North Coast two years later with husband, Richard Perkins. At that time, chose to use the Gaelic name, *Fionnaghal,* in English *Flora*, and has written and been known as Fionna Perkins ever since. Fionna has written novels, short fiction, poetry and articles. Her work is included in numerous magazines and six collections, among them: *When I Am an Old Woman I Shall Wear Purple; This Far Together, The Haight Ashbury Literary Anthology, 1980-1995; Saltwater, Sweetwater; Wood, Water, Air and Fire, The Mendocino Anthology of Women Poets.* She is one of the founders of the Coast Community Library in Point Arena.

Order Form

Floreant Press
6195 Anderson Road
Forestville, CA 95436
Telephone 707 • 887 • 7868
email: bbforest@metro.net

Please send me _____ copies of *The Horse Orchard* at $9 each.

Please include $3 shipping and handling for the first copy and $1 for each additional copy.
Californians: Please add 7.5 percent sales tax.

Name ____

Address ______________________________________

________________________________ Zip ________